DEFENDING OUR NATION

STOPPING CRIME:
THE POLICE

Series Titles

CITIZEN SOLDIERS: THE NATIONAL GUARD

CUSTOMS AND BORDER PROTECTION

DEFENDING THE SKIES: THE AIR FORCE

DEFENDING THE GROUND: THE ARMY

DEFENDING THE SEAS: THE NAVY

THE DRUG ENFORCEMENT ADMINISTRATION

HOMELAND SECURITY

THE NATIONAL COUNTERTERRORISM CENTER

PROTECTING AGAINST BIOLOGICAL AND CHEMICAL ATTACK

PUTTING OUT FIRES: FIREFIGHTERS

RESCUING HOSTAGES: THE FBI

STOPPING CRIME: THE POLICE

DEFENDING OUR NATION

STOPPING CRIME:
THE POLICE

FOREWORD BY
MANNY GOMEZ, ESQ., SECURITY AND TERRORISM EXPERT

BY
MICHAEL KERRIGAN

MASON CREST

Mason Crest
450 Parkway Drive, Suite D
Broomall, PA 19008
www.masoncrest.com

Printed in the United States of America
First printing
9 8 7 6 5 4 3 2 1

Series ISBN: 978-1-4222-3759-5
Hardcover ISBN: 978-1-4222-3771-7
ebook ISBN: 978-1-4222-8027-0

Library of Congress Cataloging-in-Publication Data

Names: Kerrigan, Michael, 1959-
Title: Stopping crime : the police / foreword by Manny Gomez, Esq., Security and Terrorism Expert ; by Michael Kerrigan.
Other titles: Police crime prevention
Description: Broomall, Pennsylvania : Mason Crest, [2018] | Series: Defending our nation | Includes index.
Identifiers: LCCN 2016053125| ISBN 9781422237717 (hardback) | ISBN
  9781422237595 (series) | ISBN 9781422280270 (ebook)
Subjects: LCSH: Crime prevention--United States--Juvenile literature. | Police--United States--Juvenile literature.
Classification: LCC HV7431 .K455 2018 | DDC 363.2/30973--dc23
LC record available at https://lccn.loc.gov/2016053125

Developed and Produced by Print Matters Productions, Inc.
(www.printmattersinc.com)
Cover and Interior Design by Bill Madrid, Madrid Design
Additional Text by Kelly Kagamas Tomkies

CONTENTS

KEY ICONS TO LOOK FOR:

Words to understand: These words with their easy-to-understand definitions will increase the reader's understanding of the text while building vocabulary skills.

Sidebars: This boxed material within the main text allows readers to build knowledge, gain insights, explore possibilities, and broaden their perspectives by weaving together additional information to provide realistic and holistic perspectives.

Educational Videos: Readers can view videos by scanning our QR codes, providing them with additional educational content to supplement the text. Examples include news coverage, moments in history, speeches, iconic sports moments and much more!

Text-dependent questions: These questions send the reader back to the text for more careful attention to the evidence presented there.

Research projects: Readers are pointed toward areas of further inquiry connected to each chapter. Suggestions are provided for projects that encourage deeper research and analysis.

Series glossary of key terms: This back-of-the book glossary contains terminology used throughout this series. Words found here increase the reader's ability to read and comprehend higher-level books and articles in this field.

FOREWORD

VIGILANCE

We live in a world where we have to have a constant state of awareness—about our surroundings and who is around us. Law enforcement and the intelligence community cannot predict or stop the next terrorist attack alone. They need the citizenry of America, of the world, to act as a force multiplier in order to help deter, detect, and ultimately defeat a terrorist attack.

Technology is ever evolving and is a great weapon in the fight against terrorism. We have facial recognition, we have technology that is able to detect electronic communications through algorithms that may be related to terrorist activity—we also have drones that could spy on communities and bomb them without them ever knowing that a drone was there and with no cost of life to us.

But ultimately it's human intelligence and inside information that will help defeat a potential attack. It's people being aware of what's going on around them: if a family member, neighbor, coworker has suddenly changed in a manner where he or she is suddenly spouting violent anti-Western rhetoric or radical Islamic fundamentalism, those who notice it have a duty to report it to authorities so that they can do a proper investigation.

In turn, the trend since 9/11 has been for international communication as well as federal and local communication. Gone are the days when law enforcement or intelligence organizations kept information to themselves and didn't dare share it for fear that it might compromise the integrity of the information or for fear that the other organization would get equal credit. So the NYPD wouldn't tell anything to the FBI, the FBI wouldn't tell the CIA, and the CIA wouldn't tell the British counterintelligence agency, MI6, as an example. Improved as things are, we could do better.

We also have to improve global propaganda. Instead of dropping bombs, drop education on individuals who are even considering joining ISIS. Education is salvation. We have the greatest production means in the world through Hollywood and so on, so why don't we match ISIS materials? We tried it once but the government itself tried to produce it. This is something that should definitely be privatized. We also need to match the energy of cyber attackers—and we need savvy youth for that.

There are numerous ways that you could help in the fight against terror—joining law enforcement, the military, or not-for-profit organizations like the Peace Corps. If making the world a safer place appeals to you, draw on your particular strengths and put them to use where they are needed. But everybody should serve and be part of this global fight against terrorism in some small way. Certainly, everybody should be a part of the fight by simply being aware of their surroundings and knowing when something is not right and acting on that sense. In the investigation after most successful attacks, we know that somebody or some persons or people knew that there was something wrong with the person or persons who perpetrated the attack. Although it feels awkward to tell the authorities that you believe somebody is acting suspicious and may be a terrorist sympathizer or even a terrorist, we have a higher duty not only to society as a whole but to our family, friends, and ultimately ourselves to do something to ultimately stop the next attack.

It's not *if* there is going to be another attack, but where, when, and how. So being vigilant and being proactive are the orders of the day.

Manny Gomez, Esq.
President of MG Security Services,
Chairman of the National Law Enforcement Association,
former FBI Special Agent, U.S. Marine, and NYPD Sergeant

CHAPTER 1
CRIME

Crimes can happen close to home or even in your home; however, there are plenty of ways to prevent them. When walking through an unknown area, be sure you're accompanied by friends.

C rime blights American society—and, indeed, many societies around the world—eating away at the fabric of our nation. In the most prosperous country on Earth, life is impoverished for many by anxiety and fear; in times of peace, crime has turned our inner cities into virtual war zones.

It is not just the horrors of large-scale **narcotrafficking** or mass-murder that make for misery. "Minor" crimes, such as vandalism, are also a major problem. How are we to tackle the problem? In recent years, police officers and **criminologists** have been considering this question in some depth and have come up with new ideas and initiatives for catching criminals. More intriguing, however, they have also been reviewing the traditional role of a "reactive" police force—which responds to a call from the community after a crime has been committed. Now,

A jobless man sits on a windowsill in a high-crime area on Chicago's South Side in 1973.

Words to Understand

Criminologists: People who study crime, criminals, or punishment of criminals.

Narcotrafficking: Smuggling and trading illegal narcotics (drugs), such as cocaine.

Utopia: Ideal or perfect world.

experts are asking whether many crimes could not be prevented in the first place, and are developing techniques and programs designed to do just that. Society needs to be able to punish criminals, but it is equally important that would-be criminals find it difficult to offend at all. For the disease of crime, prevention is better than cure.

A Problem Solved?

We love movies or novels in which police or private detectives solve crimes, but the police—and the victims of crime—know that the reality is often less satisfactory. The arrest and conviction of the criminal may come as a relief, but they are not a "solution" to the pain and misery that has been caused. They will not bring back the murder victim to a devastated family, or restore the peace of mind to a senior citizen now too afraid to venture out; nor will they rebuild the confidence of the victim of rape or other assault.

Property crimes are often seen as of secondary importance to crimes against persons. It is true that most of us would sooner suffer the loss of a material item than be badly injured. Yet, while this theory is true on its surface, the distinction does not take into account the fact that "mere" possessions are invariably invested with strong personal emotions. For example, the husband and wife whose home has been burgled may feel an all-but-physical sense of violation as they survey the mess and damage the intruders have left behind. A few dollars' worth of jewelry may represent generations of tradition for the family in which they have been handed down.

The theft erases a link with the family's past, striking a blow against that family's sense of itself. An arrest and an insurance payment will not compensate such people for their loss. Nor will the successful conviction of the criminal amount to a solution of the crime. The real triumph would be for the offense not to have taken place to begin with, and this is the goal toward which crime prevention programs are directed.

Property crimes can cause more than financial suffering, as when stolen jewelry has sentimental value.

"Prisoners in Our Own Home"

"We used to be trusting; we weren't suspicious of anyone, but now we keep our doors locked all the time," said 83-year-old Blasco Scrofano to Fernanda Santos of the *New Hampshire Eagle-Tribune*. That was before Wayne J. Cameron, 34, forced his way into the Scrofanos' home in Lawrence, NH, and beat the elderly couple with an iron crowbar. A long-term heroin addict with a string of previous convictions, Cameron left Blasco and Beatrice Scrofano in no doubt that he meant business. He hit Mr. Scrofano twice as he knelt to open the safe in which he kept jewelry and savings.

Cameron made off with $10,000 in cash and valuables, but the damage he had done to his victims was far more than monetary. "This man left me in fear," said Mrs. Scrofano, "and this is a fear that will never leave me." Cameron was eventually caught and sentenced to serve two concurrent 20-year terms, but Blasco and Beatrice feel that they, too, are doing time—always on edge, afraid to go out. "We are prisoners in our own home," said Mr. Scrofano.

Counting the Cost

A recent study conducted by David A. Anderson, Centre College's Paul G. Blazer Professor of Economics, estimates the cost of crime per year as $3.2 trillion, which is more than the cost of health care. Costs include the costs of fear and agony and private expenditures on crime prevention, such as security systems. In a **utopian** world without crime there would, for example, be no need for any money to be spent on safes—or even locks for doors and windows.

In a 2012 report from ASIS International (ASIS) and the Institute of Finance and Management (IOFM) called "The United States Security Industry: Size and Scope, Insights, Trends, and Data," the annual cost of security in the United States is $350 billion, including the use of private detectives, a practice that is increasing.

Altogether, crime costs us far more than we think—before we even consider the actual cash value of stolen property. Each year, our society spends $5.8 billion a year on medical treatment for the victims of crime—even those not directly affected feel financial pain by paying tax contributions to federal welfare programs and higher health insurance premiums.

Yet this is just the beginning. Consider, for example, what economists call the "opportunity costs" of crime—

The presence of a home security system can in itself deter burglars.

all the other things we could do with the time and money we currently commit to this problem. Anderson bases his calculations assuming a crime-free utopia, in which no one ever had to lock a house or car. He estimates we spend four minutes every day seeing to the security of our property. Multiply this by the 365 days in every year and the 200 million adults with property in the United States, and you can see how the wasted time adds up to a major cost to the economy— $89.6 billion, says Anderson.

Moreover, if criminals were working for a living, rather than making everybody else's life miserable or serving time, they could be contributing around $40 billion every year to the legitimate economy. And what of their victims? We have already considered the expense of treating them, but what of the production lost through their time off work?

The sums Anderson has calculated are staggering, although they have to be kept in perspective. None of us seriously expects to be able to live in a world without any crime. Yet, if such expenditures could never be abolished altogether, is it unrealistic to hope that they might be significantly reduced? Think of the schools, hospitals, and other services we might fund with the money saved. Or, looking at the figures another way, the savings amount to $4,118 for each American, per year.

Providing access to counseling for mental health is an important community measure to address problems before they lead to unlawful behavior.

Living in Fear?

Each year since 1999, the National Crime Prevention Council (NCPC) has conducted a survey of prevailing attitudes to discover how Americans feel about crimes in their communities. Findings for 2000, the most recent figures available, suggest that we are "safer than some of us think . . . but not as safe as we deserve to be." In a 2014 Gallup poll, 37 percent of the people who took the survey said they lived within a mile of an area in which they would feel unsafe to walk alone at night. However, most Americans (63 percent) feel safe walking alone at night in their own neighborhood or community. However, this feeling of safety was different for women than for men. Forty-five percent of women said they did not feel safe walking alone at night in their neighborhood, while 27 percent of men felt that way.

Asked about official crime prevention programs in the NCPC poll, people's responses were again contradictory. The bad news, as far as an organization like the NCPC is concerned, is that fewer people are participating—or even seem to know about—community-level crime prevention programs. The good news is that more are reporting "engagement with" their immediate neighbors, meaning that they know and talk to them. Every study to date has found that when neighbors look out for one another, the work of the criminals is that much harder and crime rates fall.

Pedestrians need well-lit streets for safe walking at night.

Community Collapse

Nationwide figures for crime may seem awesome, but fears for our own safety tend to be exaggerated. The chances of any one of us falling victim to a significant act of violence or other serious crime are, thankfully, slender. At the same time, however, while crime may not be as fearsome as we think, it may be more damaging than we realize. The sheer, daily nuisance value of apparently "trivial" offenses takes quite a toll. Graffiti, burned-out cars, broken windows—such sights as these lend a dismal, depressing prospect to many inner cities. And, according to increasing numbers of experts, these images help create the sort of climate in which crime seems unexceptional, inevitable, and therefore acceptable—particularly to the young people living in these neighborhoods.

In this, experts are following the philosophy of George L. Kelling, an emeritus professor at Rutgers University, NJ, and Fellow of the Program for Criminal Justice Policy and Management of the John F. Kennedy School of Government, Harvard. From the early 1980s onward, Kelling proposed a policy known as **zero-tolerance** policing. Taken up enthusiastically by police forces in America and worldwide, its intention is not, as some critics have suggested, to "criminalize" whole communities of largely innocent citizens, but to establish the authority of the police officer—and thus the law—on every street.

In some ways, this represents a return to old-fashioned policing values. But it is also a radical shift, turning policing priorities upside down. Kelling's criticism was that police officers were turning a blind eye to petty offenses at the street level because they felt they had more important crimes to deal with. There was neither the time nor the resources, they argued, to bother with matters like drinking in public or littering. Kelling argued that, on the contrary, law enforcement must begin with the basics. Look after these, he said, and the vast range of crime will suddenly seem more manageable.

The work of graffiti artists in the Harlem section of New York City.

A police cruiser visits Powell Street in San Francisco, CA.

A thief breaks into a car in the middle of the day.

In effect, this is a matter of simple pride. Where patrolling police officers take pride in the orderliness of a neighborhood, the people of that community are better able to maintain their own control. Where, by contrast, the little abuses are ignored, the whole neighborhood may be set for a downward slide. Kelling sketches a heart-sinking scenario, but one which is only too recognizable:

> A stable neighborhood of families who care for their homes, mind each other's children, and confidently frown on unwanted intruders can change, in a few years or even a few months, to an inhospitable and frightening jungle. A piece of property is abandoned, weeds grow up, a window is smashed. Adults stop scolding rowdy children; the children, in turn, become more rowdy. Families move out, single adults move in. Teenagers gather in front of the corner store. The merchant asks them to move; they refuse. Fights occur. Litter accumulates. People start drinking in front of the grocery; in time, a drunk slumps to the sidewalk and is allowed to sleep it off. Panhandlers approach pedestrians.

Police use new training tactics to avoid deadly shootings.

At this point, it is not inevitable that serious crime will flourish or violent attacks on strangers will occur, but many residents think that crime, especially violent crime, is on the rise, and they modify their behavior accordingly. They use the streets less often and, when on the streets, stay apart from their fellows, moving with averted eyes, silent lips, and hurried steps. 'Don't get involved'.

Kelling's work has had a profound effect on policing in recent years, but his conclusions have vast implications for citizens. Just as people need self-respect before others will respect them, so do wider communities. We all have a role to play in looking after the neighborhoods in which we live. If we do not care about litter or vandalism, why should outsiders? Crime prevention is not just about locking doors and windows, any more than crime is just about robbery, rape, or murder. Successful law enforcement starts with the individual citizen on the street.

Text-Dependent Questions
1. What is a property crime?
2. What is the estimated cost of crimes per year?
3. If criminals were working instead of committing crime, how much money would they add to the national economy?

Research Projects
1. Research to find a criminologist who helped solve a famous case. How did the criminologist solve the case? What tools did he or she use?
2. What is the most prevalent crime committed against youth ages 12 to 24? How are law enforcement agencies working to prevent these crimes?

CHAPTER 2

PREVENTION

A metropolitan police officer in Washington, DC, 1955.

C rime prevention makes no claim to be rocket science. On the contrary, it is founded in plain and practical common sense; and far from being a new idea, it is as old as crime itself. For as long as people have had possessions, they have taken trouble to keep them safe; for as long as there have been thieves, people have tried to exclude them.

While it is true that the officially coordinated crime prevention program is a relatively recent development, the underlying principles of such programs have been tried and tested over many centuries. The broken window theory is new as a sociological idea, but its essential insight into human nature is one that has been recognized from the earliest times.

William J. Bratton, as commissioner of New York City's police, followed and popularized the broken windows strategy.

Words to Understand

Juvenile delinquency: Antisocial behavior of a youth beyond parental control.

Subculture: Group that has beliefs and behaviors different from the main groups in a culture or society.

Turf: Neighborhood.

A police officer takes a report in South Central Los Angeles. Safe communities require positive relationships between neighborhood residents and law enforcement personnel.

The involvement of the police in crime prevention work is also not as innovative as it seems. Indeed, if anything, it represents a return to traditional policing values. Those who founded the first police forces never anticipated they would rush to respond to each emergency summons as it came. Rather, they saw officers patiently building security and social stability from the ground up.

Founding Principles

Humans are social animals by instinct, but that has never been a block to envy or aggression. Crime is one of the great eternals of the human condition. So, fortunately, is common sense. Crime prevention in its most primitive sense originated with the first person to hide a favorite flint blade where others would not find it. The streets of ancient Rome were as mean and murderous as those of any modern city; citizens understood that they had to take precautions to protect themselves. The essentials of common sense have never changed. Then, as now, people lock their doors and windows, avoid dark streets and alleys, and do not advertise the fact that they are carrying valuables.

Sense on the Street

Stay alert wherever you are—on the street, on public transportation, or in a mall.
- Get to know your neighborhood. If you sense something is wrong, know where you can get help—from police or a fire station, hospital, convenience store, restaurant, or public telephone.
- Avoid dark side streets at night. Also avoid shortcuts across vacant lots or parking lots at any time.
- Do not be obvious about money or jewelry. If you need to go to an automated teller machine, do it in the daytime; if you feel uneasy about people standing nearby, do not approach the machine at all.
- If you feel seriously uneasy about anything when you are out on the streets, shout good and loud!

Neither have the founding principles of good policing changed, as established in the first half of the 19th century. Sir Robert Peel, the British statesperson who inaugurated the world's first police force, took great pains to emphasize that these men were representatives of the communities they patrolled. Though they wore uniforms for ready recognition, he was anxious that they should not seem set apart from the people among whom they moved. "The police are the public," he insisted, "and the public are the police."

Like their English models, the first U.S. police officers in the 1840s walked routes, or "beats," which they came to know extremely well—if, that is, they did not already know them. They were naturally close to their communities, able to recognize the faces and know about local gossip—and as a result, their communities felt close to them.

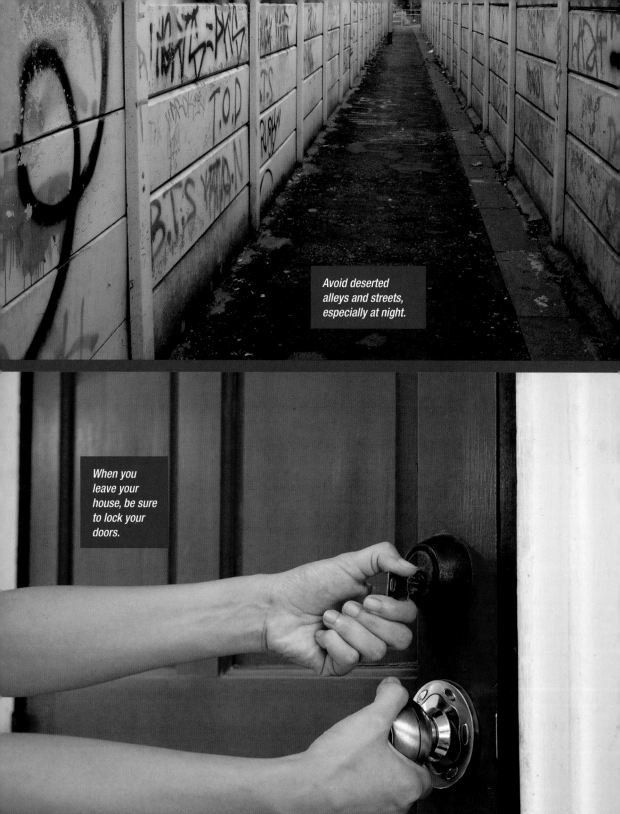

Avoid deserted alleys and streets, especially at night.

When you leave your house, be sure to lock your doors.

Boys admire the horses of the Chicago Police Department in 1941.

Through much of the 20th century, however, police forces became increasingly professional and increasingly remote from a public whose sense of involvement in law and order was fast diminishing. It was an age of specialization, and police certainly needed the new skills and experience they were acquiring, for they now had to deal with organized crime and other large-scale problems. But the public was specializing, too, with people getting increasingly wrapped up in their jobs and cut off from their communities. A new breed of suburban commuters emerged who spent hardly any time in their home neighborhoods and who scarcely knew their neighbors. Most Americans were content to just abide by the law, with no sense that any more active engagement with the wider community might be required. Concerned citizens knew to call the police when a crime took place, but that was the limit of their responsibilities.

> **Face to Face**
>
> In Wagga Wagga, a small city in New South Wales, Australia, police were concerned about the numbers of young men drifting by degrees into ever-more serious crime. At the same time, they believed victims felt that their sufferings were not recognized. Both were problems that needed to be addressed.
>
> In an imaginative program, police officers arranged meetings between offending youths and their victims, to help young criminals appreciate that their actions had consequences, which often caused other people pain. The victims, for their part, felt that for the first time their experiences were recognized.
>
> In days gone by, police officers were "community cops" who knew all the young people on their beats and who could offer informal advice and warnings from an early stage. They also knew the victims of crime, who appreciated their concern. Today, it takes an official program to recapture something of that old closeness, but it has certainly proved effective—with scores of satisfied victims and a 74 percent drop in youth crime.

As both police and public were becoming ever more removed from their home communities, it was only criminals who were remaining loyal to their home **turf**. Day in and day out, most crime was still taking place on a small scale at a local level—and neither the police nor the public were well placed to respond.

Neighborhood Watch

As the 20th century evolved, the distance grew between police departments and the communities they served—and after World War II, it did so at an even greater rate. Cruising in cars and communicating with radios, officers were able to respond to any call at a moment's notice—but they were unable to do the patient meeting and greeting that builds relationships with their local community. Women joined the workforce—and joined their husbands on the morning train to the city—meaning that more homes were left unattended.

The crime prevention programs that sprang up toward the end of the 20th century were attempts to rebuild the bond between members of the public and the police that had been broken. As early as 1972, police chiefs and sheriffs understood the importance of good neighborly practice in discouraging crime. Stark differences in crime rates were reported between districts where people did report suspicions to law enforcement officers and districts where they did not. And this was not just about a readiness to call the police, experts surmised— surely that single statistic also represented a whole set of associated attitudes and local conditions.

In short, there was one sort of community where neighbors looked out for each other, and there was a second in which they told themselves, "It's not my problem." Programs were introduced, and over the next few years, these would evolve into Neighborhood Watch. The effects were dramatic and almost immediate. Burglaries in areas where the program was introduced fell by up to 75 percent. Not surprisingly, the program was quickly broadened in scope.

Neighborhood Watch signs placed throughout neighborhoods let residents and potential criminals know the area is organized and serious about preventing crime.

Since then, Neighborhood Watch and similar programs have flourished, helped by promotional campaigns, like that of the National Crime Prevention Council (NCPC) and Crime Prevention Coalition of America (CPCA). Local police forces spearhead these nationwide initiatives, aimed at recruiting ordinary people into the fight against crime.

These campaigns drive home the same message as Sir Robert Peel: that the police and the public are one and the same, or that, as today's slogan puts it, crime prevention is "everybody's business."

This is often a difficult message to get to young people, who tend to resent any authority, particularly that of the police; their **subculture** may even encourage suspicion of

Police yellow tape cordons off smoldering remains of a local business in Ferguson, MO, in the aftermath of riots over news that a police officer who killed an unarmed black teenager would not face charges.

authority. Yet many police officers are young themselves and share the enthusiasms of other young people. This recognition led the police department of Dayton, OH, to establish COP'RZ, while Middletown, CT, has its Blue Crew. These rap and rock groups perform at young people's parties, bringing together two communities who have often been at odds.

Gradually, the bond between police and the public is being renewed. The police are regaining some of the detailed understanding of local communities that their predecessors once had, and this in turn is cutting crime. A good example of this comes from Merseyside, England, where a "crime-mapping" program was established in 1995. Assembling information on places where multiple offenses have taken place, police identified particular hot spots in areas already high in crime. Investment was then focused on those places in different forms—everything from the fitting of locks, lighting, and alarms to job training and sports programs for young offenders. Since the program began, emergency calls to the police have dropped by as much as 20 percent, cutting costs and cutting crime.

How to start a Neighborhood Watch program.

As the work of the police is seen to have an effect and the public regains its trust, the only losers are criminals. But this is a process without end, and it calls for imagination and goodwill, both now and in the future. The bond between the police and the public can be strengthened, but each side must be prepared to go out and meet the other halfway to rebuild our communities.

On the Move

Soldiers patrol train station platforms in Lille, France.

During 1990, 840 million people made journeys by train in France, and 968 acts of violence on trains were committed. That ratio, in fact, makes rail travel in the country comparatively safe—but this was not the perception of the public in Paris. A major urban center, Paris has had all the usual big-city problems: travelers on its trains had to contend with everything from vandalism to vagrants. Again, actual violence was infrequent, but as George L. Kelling has pointed out, the perception of violence can be a profoundly damaging problem, since it creates the conditions in which violence is more liable to flourish.

Thus those who could afford to do so—usually young, middle-class commuters—started finding other ways of traveling, and the rail network was left to the homeless and the criminal and to those who had no other means of transportation. The city's elderly felt especially vulnerable. The response of the authorities was twofold. First, they took active steps to improve safety on the system, with extra station staff, video surveillance, and panic alarms. They also supported social service programs aimed at integrating homeless people into Paris life and tackling juvenile delinquency.

Black Lives Matter demonstrators across the United States focus on holding police accountable for unjustified violence.

From the early days of professional policing, ensuring the positive role of patrol officers in communities has been a challenge. In this 1892 newspaper illustration, Thomas Nash, a famous cartoonist of the time, takes a poke at police corruption.

Text-Dependent Questions

1. Who inaugurated the world's first police force? When?
2. What is a Neighborhood Watch group and what does the group do?
3. What was one effect of a Neighborhood Watch Group?

Research Projects

1. Research a Neighborhood Watch Group near you. How many people are involved? How do people get involved? How has the group affected crime in that area?
2. Research the National Crime Prevention Council. What is its mission? How does it accomplish this mission?

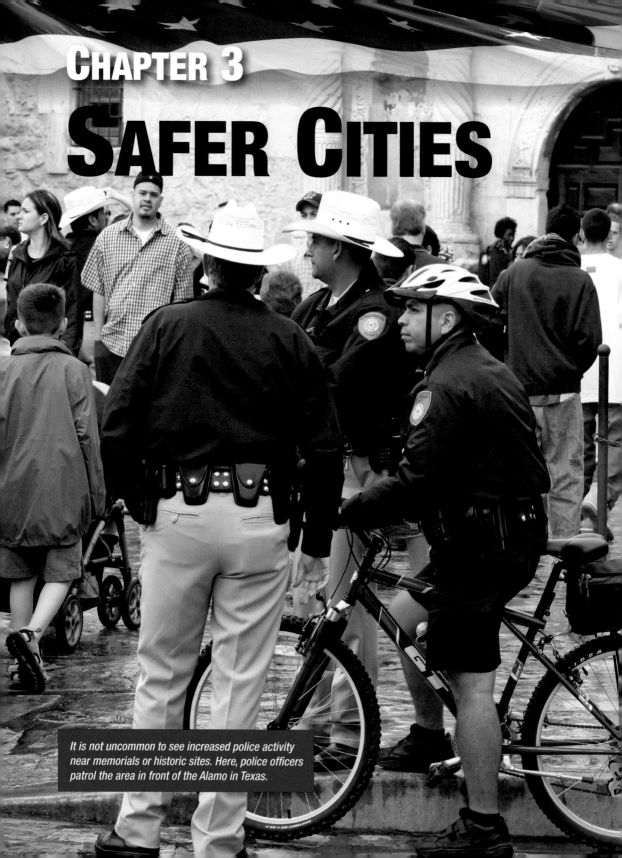

CHAPTER 3
SAFER CITIES

It is not uncommon to see increased police activity near memorials or historic sites. Here, police officers patrol the area in front of the Alamo in Texas.

I n discussing the work of crime prevention programs, there is little point in concentrating on theory: these programs must work in practice, or they are no use at all. Although there are associated theories—the broken window theory, for example—these have been tested for so long and so rigorously that they are now considered common sense.

It is also important to remember that truly creative crime prevention thinking does not rely on just one theory. Rather, it approaches the problem from many different directions. Increased police presence, video surveillance, alarms, working with offenders, working with victims and would-be victims, repairs to street lamps, litter patrols, visits to day care centers and schools: a typical crime prevention program can involve all these things and more. A number of different

Police–community relations are on the upswing in Fort Worth, TX, where traffic stops don't always involve motorists.

Words to Understand

Hierarchy: Levels of status or control within a group.

Punitive: Intended to punish someone or something.

Truancy: The state of being absent from school without permission.

agencies, as well as the public, work together in the drive for a safer neighborhood and a higher quality of life.

This chapter focuses on one American city, looking at the ways its police and people tackled a crime problem that at one point seemed overwhelming. It has by no means been clear sailing all the way, nor could it be claimed that the war against crime has definitely been won, but the people of Fort Worth, TX, feel strongly that their efforts have been worthwhile.

Prevention Pioneers

Fort Worth, TX, takes pride in being "the city where the West begins." It recently became home to the National Cowgirl Museum and Hall of Fame. A successful tourist industry has been built upon its fascinating history of the frontier days, and visitors come from all over the world to see the world's only daily cattle drive in the city stockyards.

In addition to the rough romance of the old West, tourists are also drawn to Fort Worth by other attractions, particularly its world-famous Modern Art Museum, the biggest gallery of modern art outside New York. In truth, neither tourists nor Fort Worth's half-million population have felt any desire to experience Wild West–style lawlessness firsthand. By the mid-1980s, however, many citizens were finding their quality of life seriously affected by both the fear and the reality of crime, due mostly to the crack cocaine market.

Partnership

Fort Worth was not alone in its problems. Other Texan cities were affected, which prompted the launch in 1992 of an initiative known as T-CAP. The Texas City Action Plan to Prevent Crime involved not only Fort Worth but also Arlington, Austin, Corpus Christi, Dallas, Houston, and San Antonio. A partnership between seven cities, T-CAP encouraged and facilitated coordination and consultation between politicians, police departments, and public service agencies across the state; more importantly, however, it also encouraged partnership within member communities.

The idea that if one broken window in a building is neglected, others will soon be broken too, is the basis of the broken window theory of policing.

All manner of agencies in Fort Worth have been involved in the program, from the police to educators, from housing authorities to healthcare workers. Indeed, participation extends all the way down the city **hierarchy** to pest control, for no detail is too small as is shown by the broken window theory. Local businesses are also involved, from major companies to corner stores: all have come together with ordinary citizens to discuss how their needs might best be served.

The involvement of as many individuals and interest groups as possible is, of course, important as a matter of democratic principle—but it serves another highly practical purpose too. The more people feel that they are being consulted and that they have a voice in running their community, the more they will take pride in it and defend it. Is an act of vandalism just "one of those things"? Is a pile of litter to be dismissed as "someone else's problem"? Or are both to be resented as affronts to the community at large? How they are regarded depends on how much individual residents feel involved: is the neighborhood their home—or just some place where they have ended up living?

Graffiti Wars

It may seem a minor problem, but graffiti is unsightly and is also depressing. Whatever the actual words, the meaning between the lines is clear: "We don't care how our neighborhood looks." That message, in turn, leads to acts of more serious vandalism and petty crime. Before you know it, a nice street is on the slide. But if graffiti is often the beginning of social disintegration for an entire neighborhood, it is also often an early step in a young offender's journey toward crime. There are two good reasons, then, for tackling graffiti as soon as it appears.

Battling Narcotics

Like many other large communities, Fort Worth has been waging war against the sale and use of narcotics for decades. As of 2016, its Narcotics Section comprises more than 50 officers. The primary drug it battles: crack cocaine.

Fort Worth's Narcotics section has expanded from primarily covert operations to educating children, health professionals, and religious and citizen groups. The section also focuses on street level narcotic enforcement and illegal distribution of prescription drugs. These active professionals also often partner with the Drug Enforcement Administration and the Federal Bureau of Investigation to take drugs and drug dealers off the streets of Fort Worth.

In Laval, QC, Canada, police and courts have worked alongside city school boards, shops, and businesses in trying to clamp down on graffiti. Young offenders have been vigorously pursued and prosecuted, and they have also been required in many cases to repair the damage themselves. Shopkeepers and residents are encouraged to report offenses. One of the difficulties with what are perceived to be "minor" crimes is that people start taking them for granted. In effect, the crime is accepted, taking the whole neighborhood another step down the slippery slope that can eventually lead to complete breakdown in law and order.

McGruff the Crime Dog from the National Crime Prevention Council visits schoolchildren.

In a program in Haarlem in the Netherlands, a unique solution was found to this problem. The Schwarbroek Tunnel was, in theory, a right of way for pedestrians and cyclists, but few people ventured near, fearing it as a dark and dangerous haunt of violent youth gangs. In 1994, the local government took action, cleaning the tunnel completely and installing new lighting. The city's Linnaeus College then "adopted" the tunnel as a gallery for youth art, displaying the energy and creativity of Haarlem youngsters. Nor was this a one-time program. The Schwarbroek has a regularly changing calendar of events, just like any other art museum. General use of the tunnel has stayed high, which in turn has helped keep vandals at bay; there has been little new graffiti in the last few years.

Safety

In Fort Worth, T-CAP considered every aspect of safety in the city, not just security from criminal attack. Thus the Fort Worth Police Department worked with the housing authority on a traffic plan to enhance road safety, while city government was pressed to provide better street lighting as a guard against both accidents and crime. This is an instance of a theory known as CPTED (pronounced "sep-ted")—Crime Prevention Through Environmental Design.

It sounds sophisticated, but CPTED has a core of common sense. The idea is that city planners, architects, and landscapers can program security into their designs from

CPTED has worked to make public spaces, like this illuminated basketball court, feel safe again.

the very start, designing buildings and public spaces in which people will feel safe (and criminals will feel uncomfortable). Is that underpass well lit, or is it dark and threatening? Are the approaches open and inviting, or are there shadowy bushes or concrete angles where muggers may lurk? A path across an open area will feel a lot safer if a busy public basketball court has been placed nearby. When people feel safe and confident that the streets are their own and the more the public feels in control, the less that criminals feel they have a scope for action. The purpose of CPTED is to make the reduction of criminal activity a basic objective of planning and design. Broadcasting classical music in alleys and around convenience stores has also been used to move juveniles out of areas.

Beating the Bullies

Studies in the 1980s revealed that 9 percent of schoolchildren in Norway were bullied. This was bad news, not only for them but also for their country, as statistics also showed that those 7 percent of students who were picking on their classmates were four times more likely to become criminals as adults.

Rather than intervening aggressively, the Norwegian authorities decided on a large-scale campaign of education. An advice booklet was issued to teachers, and every parent with a school-age child was given a folder with information and advice about the problem. A video offering additional advice was available for anyone who asked, and the situation was monitored by means of questionnaires. Children were asked about their own experiences of bullying, if any, and the readiness of teachers and fellow students to help. Although there was no punitive campaign against the bullies, the issue was kept "live." At the end of two years, the number of bullying victims had fallen by 50 percent, and there were indications that vandalism, theft, and truancy had also fallen.

T-CAP also sponsored self-defense workshops to give citizens more confidence on the streets. Local laws and regulations were reviewed and rationalized in consultation between the police and the housing authority. One outcome was the banning of glass bottles, for reasons of general safety. It is a minor innovation, but when combined with many others, it can add up to a wholesale change in the quality of life.

A group marching in the annual LGBT pride parade in Vancouver, BC, Canada, carries an "erase bullying" banner.

Education

Education is also a priority. In Fort Worth, this went beyond lecturing schoolchildren on the evils of crime. Local businesses were encouraged to provide scholarships and support for school activities. This promoted pride within the community, boosting not just the lucky students themselves but also their families, neighbors, and classmates. And it gave students from disadvantaged backgrounds a reason to strive. It also had the effect of binding those businesses to the communities in which they were established. Previously, these businesses may not have felt any such ties, having forgotten perhaps that communities do not stop existing outside office hours. T-CAP also encouraged the adoption of school uniforms—a move that has proven time and again to encourage discipline and pride. It also promoted the idea of year-round schooling with several electives to discourage idleness and to lower dropout rates.

A family discusses crime prevention with a member of the Los Angeles County Sherriff's Department at a National Night Out against crime community fair.

Police have a part to play in education too—both in the straightforward sense that they can act as "teachers," offering students the benefit of their experience, and in the sense that school visits provide an opportunity for the police to meet and form a relationship with younger people. Under T-CAP, existing DARE (Drug Abuse Resistance Education) programs were expanded.

Adopt a Cop

Police in Queensland, Australia, have an interesting way of getting their message into schools. Children "adopt" an officer from their local force for regular visits throughout their time at school. Talking with children on subjects from drug abuse to road safety, and from what to do when approached by strangers to the basics of home security, officers give these children vital tips on protecting themselves. Older students discuss issues such as actions and consequences and rights and responsibilities.

Perhaps as important as the content of these lessons, however, is the fact that children find themselves encountering a police officer in a caring, friendly role. This opens a line of communication between police and young people, and this, it is hoped, will endure into their teenage years and beyond.

When young people have places for recreation, communities are safer.

Young and Old

Education is for parents too. T-CAP initiated programs to involve them more closely with the running of their children's schools and provided help with childcare to enable them to be more effective parents. "Safe Houses" were opened to give children a safe place to play after school while parents were at work, and there were programs to train more qualified childcare providers.

For the elderly, special programs offered a range of trips and activities, which brought together young people and senior citizens. The young may often regard the elderly with a mixture of contempt and resentment; the old frequently view the young with cynicism and fear. Neither prejudice is fair, as many participants in T-CAP Fort Worth found, to their real pleasure. An "Adopt a Senior" program established special, and often mutually supportive, relationships between young people and elderly neighbors, to the advantage of both sides—and, indeed, the whole community.

Steps you can take to stop bullying.

Busy Vacations

"The Devil finds work for idle hands." Whoever originated that expression could easily have been thinking of the long summer vacation; trouble always seems to find some way of thriving in those endless, empty weeks. In France, local government offers young people in disadvantaged suburbs the opportunity to take part in all sorts of special programs: mainly sports and community activities, but also artistic and educational ones. The program started in 1981 in the city of Lyon in response to one particularly "long, hot summer" in which serious violence flared up among gangs of idle teenagers. It proved such a success that the program was soon adopted throughout the whole of France—and not just during summer, but all significant school vacations.

A Force for Change

Having encouraged so many citizens, local government, and businesses to change their attitudes and approaches, the Fort Worth Police Department could hardly exclude itself from the need to institute initiatives and reforms. In fact, change was little short of revolutionary. The police department serves an area that covers 353 square miles (914 sq km). This was divided into five patrol divisions (Central, East, North, South, West) in an effort to enable police work to return to its roots in the local communities. These divisions are overseen by two commands. North Command oversees Central, West, and North patrol divisions, while South Command oversees East, South, and Traffic divisions.

Text-Dependent Questions

1. What is T-CAP?
2. What is CPTED and how does it work?
3. Name one initiative T-CAP launched aimed to improve the lives of youth.

Research Projects

1. Research a local DARE program. What is its mission? How often do officers speak at schools and other organizations? How many people have seen a presentation?
2. What does your local police department do to protect elderly people in your community? Does it have special programs?

CHAPTER 4

POLICING SMALL TOWNS

Communities do their part every day to protect their homes and families.

W hen we think of an American small town, we think of a quiet and contented community free from crime. Here, everyone knows one another; here, there is true community spirit; here, you do not even need to think of locking your front door. That, at any rate, is the myth. Now, let us take a look at the reality.

It is true that such communities avoid some of the problems of big-city life. It is equally true, however, that it takes more than a white picket fence to keep out crime. There have always been vagrants and delinquents around who upset the peacefulness of small-town life. And in recent generations, the most far-flung country areas have been subject to many of the same social pressures as the big cities: family breakups, teenage drinking, drugs, and gangs.

The scale of the problem is often exaggerated—as it is in the urban centers—but there is no doubt that crime is now an everyday part of rural and small-town life in every part of the United States. Here, too, Americans have had to organize their own community-based crime prevention programs, also encouraged and led by local law enforcement agencies.

For a Crime-Free Freeport

The smaller communities of America were once a byword for quiet coziness, but they are not feeling quite so comfortable now. With a population of some 24,000, Freeport, in northwestern Illinois, is the sort of small town in which generations of city-dwelling Americans have dreamed of living. Even here, however, people have recently felt the need to mount resistance against rising rates of crime. By 1994, there was a sense that youth crime was beginning to spiral. The

Words to Understand

Enterprising: Having or showing the desire to do new and difficult things.

Trespassing: Crime of going on someone's land without permission.

Unscrupulous: Not honest or fair.

This raided methamphetamine lab in Barren County, KY, is one of thousands that have sprung up throughout the United States.

wider community looked on, feeling powerless to intervene. Much of the reported crime was "minor"—vandalism and rowdiness, for example. Nonetheless, it contributed to a growing feeling of insecurity among the population at large and a steadily diminishing quality of life. In 1994, local police, politicians, officials, and residents came together to form the Freeport Coalition for a Safe Community, with its mission "to build a safe and healthy community for our children and families." Since this time, the coalition has disbanded, but the efforts to improve public safety have not. Freeport Mayor, Jim Gitz, worked with police in 2014 to create a public safety plan.

At the center of the plan was a drive to establish new Neighborhood Watch groups, bringing householders together with one another and with the police in the fight against crime. The city also tore down abandoned buildings, approved a rental property ordinance with a crime-free housing addendum, passed a parental responsibility law, enforced its curfew law, and started reaching out to neighborhoods to meet crime prevention needs.

According to the mayor, these efforts have seen results. Incidents of aggravated battery, battery, motor vehicle burglary, and residential burglary have dropped significantly since 2012, the year before the changes began. While Mayor Gitz admits not all statistics (for example, retail burglary) have improved, it is clear that the concentrated combined efforts of police and residents is having the desired effect.

The Virginia Version

Not all crime prevention programs need to be community based, although all need the cooperation of the people among whom they are launched. Some may be initiatives of the local police.

In one past program, the Virginia State Police were resourceful in tackling particular crime prevention problems in their own, largely rural, policing area. One of these, Rest Area Watch, was mounted in response to an escalating problem of crime at the state's roadside rest areas—a number of violent, in some cases homicidal, attacks were made at these isolated sites.

In a well-publicized campaign, patrolling officers made regular checks on rest areas. Critics said it was a lot of fuss and fanfare for what amounted to just a few minutes' policing time each day, but publicity is an important part of policing. If only one criminal sees the news on TV and decides it is no longer worth the risk, then crimes have been prevented and—very possibly—lives have been saved. Virginia's police officers are well satisfied with the program. Figures show a clear drop in this type of crime. Hence, the inauguration of similar programs: Convenience Store Watch and Worship Watch (based around local stores, churches, and other places of worship), in which special patrols have been established and advice on CPTED (Crime Prevention Through Environmental Design) issues given.

REST AREA PATROLLED BY STATE POLICE

FOR EMERGENCY CALL
1-800-XXX-XXXX
CELLULAR #77

Road sign used in the state of Virginia at a rest area.

A Brake on Drunk Driving

Breathalyzers, which measure how drunk people are, play an important role in punishing and preventing drunk driving.

For many years, drunk driving was not recognized as a crime. Since the offense is so often committed by members of the public who would never dream of breaking other laws, it has taken generations for police to instill the idea that it is indeed a crime—and a dangerous crime at that.

Increasingly, more and more young people are committing this crime. The 16–24 age group was responsible for an appalling 54 percent of America's alcohol-related nighttime fatal crashes in 2009, and for teenagers, drunk driving is the leading cause of death.

Students Against Driving Drunk (SADD)—the name was later modified to Students Against Destructive Decisions—was set up in Wayland, MA, in 1981. The aim was to unite students and their parents against a problem that was taking lives both young and old. At the center of SADD's philosophy is the Contract for Life, in which parents and students agree never to drive after drinking and to give each other rides when either is "above the limit."

Country Crime

Many Americans, living in big cities, find it hard to believe there could be any such thing as rural crime: surely life is always wonderfully quiet and peaceful in country areas! Rural dwellers know better: they may be spared the more spectacular gang-related violence of the more notorious inner-city areas, but in other respects they suffer much the same as their fellow citizens.

Vandalism, burglary, auto-related crime, drunk driving: such crimes have all helped blight the rural idyll in recent decades. In addition, farming folk must contend with problems their urban counterparts never dreamt of facing. Straight from the semimythical days of the Old West, for example, comes the all-too-real

Oklahoma police catch crystal meth addicts stealing cattle for money.

A coal train slips into a once-prosperous West Virginia town. Where jobs are scarce, crime soon follows.

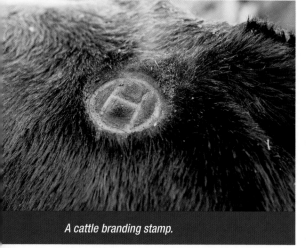
A cattle branding stamp.

crime of cattle rustling—as grave a problem as it ever was in John Wayne's day, but not half so romantic.

Today's rustlers are more likely to drive 18-wheeler trucks than to ride ponies, and their motivation would have meant little to the more colorful outlaws of former times. Reporting on the problem for Statewide TV, Nebraska, Bill Kelly sums up the situation with depressing frankness: "No one really wants to admit just how easy it is to steal someone else's cattle. In a matter of minutes it can earn an **enterprising** thief more money than holding up a convenience store and with a lot less hassle."

Watchers of old-fashioned Western movies will be well aware of the time-honored tradition of "branding" cattle—of literally burning an owner's mark into the hide of a calf with a red-hot metal stamp. The brand stays with the animal as it grows: attempts to tamper with it are usually apparent, and it certainly cannot be removed, so the system allows the effective registration of America's entire livestock herd. Substantially the same method is used for branding as is to be seen in the old movies; now, however, it is backed up with a carefully managed system of state and nationwide record keeping, all strictly policed by a designated force of "Brand Inspectors."

In theory, then, the origins and ownership of any animal can be checked by a potential buyer as readily as those of any secondhand car; in practice, of course, things are not necessarily quite so straightforward. An **unscrupulous** rancher may well feel the risks of detection are worth running in light of the profits to be made from keeping stolen stock—whereas yet unbranded young calves are involved those risks become virtually nonexistent. Not surprisingly, there is a lucrative "black market" in unmarked animals like this, each of which may be worth $2,000 or more.

Stealing the brand—cattle theft.

Rural Crime Unit

Rural crime prevention is the goal of the California Rural Crimes Prevention Task Force (CRCPTF). The CRCPTF accomplishes its goal through a combination of education and communication across the state. The leadership of the organization is made up of representatives from four major counties in California: San Bernardino, Tehama, Sonoma, and Kern. Members include law enforcement agencies, government agencies, and industry partners.

Typical crimes CRCPTF has sought to prevent are those many rural communities face: animal fighting, **trespassing**, metal theft, livestock theft, and heavy equipment theft, among others.

Perhaps the most important benefit to being a member of the CRCPTF is its Rural Crime School. Held annually, it is a way for members to gain expertise in rural crime. It is designed for patrol officers, investigators, regulators, and crime prevention personnel.

Text-Dependent Questions

1. What organization in Freeport, IL, helped the community prevent crime in 1994?
2. What state instituted a program to patrol rest areas to prevent crimes there?
3. What is the goal of the California Rural Crimes Prevention Task Force?

Research Projects

1. Select a small town near you. Research to discover if it has any special crime prevention programs. If so, what are they and what people and organizations are involved?
2. Research to discover what the most common crime is in a rural region near you.

CHAPTER 5

DOMESTIC CRIME

Getting people to report domestic crime is one of the biggest challenges to stopping it.

C rime prevention officers spend much of their time advising householders how to secure their homes against intruders. But when you have locked all the doors and windows, have you excluded all possible dangers? Sadly, in too many households, the answer is no. Domestic violence and child abuse can make a home a place of suffering.

Unfortunately, society is just now starting to comprehend the scale and seriousness of these crimes. Police forces are only now learning how to tackle such difficult offenses.

Under Lock and Key

The most imaginative program in the world cannot substitute for basic precautions, and police forces throughout America spend much of their time advising householders on

ways of making their homes and vehicles secure. Double-mortise locks to ensure firm front doors, peepholes and chains for checking callers, locks on windows, and timer-operated lights to make an empty house look occupied—there are lots of ways in which you can make a home a less-inviting target for the criminal. Immobilizers, alarms, and tracking devices help safeguard a car. Crime prevention officers provide information and advice on all these measures.

Security cameras are used by businesses and homeowners to deter criminal activity.

Words to Understand

Controversial: Causing much discussion, disagreement, or argument.

Sexism: Prejudice or discrimination based on sex, especially discrimination against women.

Undermine: Make someone or something weaker.

Behind Closed Doors

The home is not just a target of crime. In many cases, it is the source. Domestic violence and child abuse are a continuing problem in every part of the United States and in every social class. Partner violence has been described as a hidden crime. Not only is it characteristically

Combatting domestic violence.

committed in the privacy of the home, it is an area in which law enforcement has traditionally been reluctant to get involved. **Sexism** was a factor for a long time, of course. A predominantly male police force was, at times, too quick to discount the claims of women victims, or was too willing to see men's version of events. Sometimes, women made accusations and then withdrew them, or refused to acknowledge when violence was only too clearly going on. Police were, therefore, wary of involving themselves in investigations that often proved a waste of everyone's time.

Today, we have a better understanding of the sort of situations in which domestic violence takes place, and the often crushing pressures that prevent many victims from acting in their own defense. Fears of the violent partner contend with reluctance to acknowledge the failure of the relationship as well as fears about financial disruption that may follow a breakup due to invoking the law. There may be complicating input, too, from in-laws and from friends—not to mention the attacker's insistence that, this time, he really will change. The recruitment of thousands of women to the police force has helped, as have the education of officers and the many campaigns promising victims support if they come forward.

A memorial in downtown Ottawa, ON, Canada's Minto Park remembers women abused and murdered by men.

Sisters in Law

Like many other countries around the world, Brazil has had a long history of domestic violence and its police a shameful record of indifference toward a "private" matter. The reluctance of women to complain was reinforced by the contempt they received from the police if they tried to do so—which effectively gave the green light to continued violence.

Urged on by the State Council for the Status of Women, the authorities finally acted. The first of a series of all-women police stations was opened in São Paulo in 1985 to provide a reassuring environment for victims of violence. As well as offering sympathy, the women officers bring special experience to bear, as well as psychological help and—when needed—emergency shelter. Counseling is provided to male perpetrators of violence. Practice suggests that men find it easier to accept such help from women.

As with all crime prevention programs, one of its benefits is the signal it sends to the wider community. The opening of the women's police station—and of several others like it since—has made it clear that domestic violence is a serious issue. Indeed, there are encouraging signs that the new stations have had a major impact, both in cutting crime and in changing attitudes. Femicide, a sex-based hate crime against a woman, was made illegal in Brazil in 2015.

Breaking the Cycle

The Elmira Police Department in New York State has, along with many others across America, a busy Victims' Services Unit. Its trained officers offer advice and support to those who have suffered all sorts of violent crime, but they have a special role in assisting those who have already been victims of domestic violence.

While no one would dispute that this sort of after-the-fact help is beneficial, can it really be described as crime prevention? Elmira officers are adamant that it can. Domestic violence, unfortunately, is seldom a one-time offense. Almost invariably, it is a long and ever-deepening cycle. In Britain, where two women a week are killed by their partners, a recent survey showed that victims had been beaten an average of 35 times before they finally reported their

The Pringle-Patric House in Springfield, OH, built in 1877, was converted into a shelter for abused women.

problems to the police. A timely intervention at an early stage can help prevent a whole succession of future crimes—including, perhaps, the crime of murder. Also in Elmira, there has been a determined drive by health care and social services to assist disadvantaged teenaged mothers with support during pregnancy and the early years of child rearing. Since 1978, visits by nurses have helped not only with health issues but also with other aspects of parenting. This is clearly an admirable program, but, again, what does it have to do with crime prevention? In fact, it has consistently been shown that neglected or abused children are more likely to turn to crime in later life. Elmira has done itself a favor by this act of community kindness. There has been a 66 percent drop in the arrest rate among those teenagers who passed through the program.

This sign is part of a campaign against domestic violence in Uganda, Africa.

Suffer the Little Children—and the Elderly Too

Children themselves are often victims of violence, of course—and even witnessing attacks on others can be profoundly traumatic: there is mounting evidence that such experiences can lead to the sort of psychological disturbance that tends to lead in its turn to violence and crime. Police in New Haven, CT, have been working with psychologists at the city's Yale University in an interesting new program that attempts to address this problem. Basically, mental health professionals and police officers have been comparing notes and sharing skills, enabling both to build a more psychologically sensitive approach to community policing together.

Attacks upon children by grown-ups not known to them are, in fact, comparatively rare, however large they may loom in the imaginations of anxious parents. But they can occur in reality, of course, and they are peculiarly distressing when they do; hence the need to instruct children in how they should respond to approaches from strangers. The message is simple enough, but it has to be driven home anew for every generation of children—who are naturally trusting. Be wary of attention from any adult not personally known to you—however nice or "cool" he or she may seem—and on no account get into a stranger's car. Registration programs run by police and other law-enforcement departments have played an important role in keeping such offenses to a minimum, although they can always be evaded by a determined criminal. In response, some states and cities have passed laws demanding that parents be informed if any convicted child molester moves into their neighborhood, although this sort of program is **controversial**. Opponents point to the violation of the offender's civil rights, the difficulty he may have in reforming his life in an atmosphere of hate and suspicion—and, indeed, the risk that a "lynch mob" atmosphere may create greater dangers by driving convicted abusers completely underground. Advocates argue that the safety of children must override all other rights, and that more is to be gained than lost in openness on this issue. In addition to registering offenders, Albuquerque, NM, registers children as well, so as to facilitate matters should the worst happen and they disappear.

Police officers visit schools to talk to students about crime prevention.

Yet many experts in the field are concerned about the emphasis given to "stranger danger" given that an estimated 80 percent of child sexual abuse is committed by relations and acquaintances of the family. Public panic about the tiny number of media "monsters," they suggest, may be blinding us to the damage being done day in, day out to countless thousands of American children by apparently ordinary and decent parents, stepparents, babysitters, and family "friends." Such attacks may not involve headline-grabbing violence, but they create real terror and **undermine** self-esteem, and they rob many victims of any hope of a happy grown-up life. Cynically exploiting as they do the child's natural instinct to trust and love, these abuses may well destroy emotional responses the growing individual will need if he or she is to form strong and enduring relationships in adulthood. Increasingly, we are waking up to the need to educate children out of an ignorance we once—quite mistakenly—prized as innocence, equipping them to recognize inappropriate behavior and to report any uneasiness they may feel to a parent or caregiver. Listening is vital.

But children are not the only ones at risk: the police department in Burlington, CA, is one of many police departments across the country making efforts to combat the growing (or perhaps only increasingly acknowledged) problem of elder abuse. The term *elder abuse* may cover anything from neglect on the part of relatives or caregivers to outright torture of the cruelest kind. Burlington officers are on the lookout for a range of warning signs, from physical bruising to psychological distress—or reluctance on the part of family or caregivers to allow the victim to be left alone with outside visitors. Listening is once again key: that old people may genuinely suffer from confusion has made it only too easy for their complaints of mistreatment to go unheeded.

Abuse of the elderly is a serious issue that is starting to be recognized and addressed openly.

Text-Dependent Questions

1. What is domestic abuse?
2. What does a Victims' Services Unit do?
3. What percent of child sexual abuse is committed by relations and acquaintances of the family?

Research Projects

1. Research to discover how often elder abuse occurs in your community. What efforts are being made by law enforcement and other community agencies to prevent it?
2. What resources are available to victims of domestic abuse in your community? How do victims access these resources?

Series Glosssary

Air marshal: Armed guard traveling on an aircraft to protect the passengers and crew; the air marshal is often disguised as a passenger.

Annexation: To incorporate a country or other territory within the domain of a state.

Armory: A supply of arms for defense or attack.

Assassinate: To murder by sudden or secret attack, usually for impersonal reasons.

Ballistic: Of or relating to firearms.

Biological warfare: Also known as germ warfare, this is war fought with biotoxins—harmful bacteria or viruses that are artificially propagated and deliberately dispersed to spread sickness among an enemy.

Cartel: A combination of groups with a common action or goal.

Chemical warfare: The use of poisonous or corrosive substances to kill or incapacitate the enemy; it differs from biological warfare in that the chemicals concerned are not organic, living germs.

Cold War: A long and bitter enmity between the United States and the Free World and the Soviet Union and its Communist satellites, which went on from 1945 to the collapse of Communism in 1989.

Communism: A system of government in which a single authoritarian party controls state-owned means of production.

Conscription: Compulsory enrollment of persons especially for military service.

Consignment: A shipment of goods or weapons.

Contingency operations: Operations of a short duration and most often performed at short notice, such as dropping supplies into a combat zone.

Counterintelligence: Activities designed to collect information about enemy espionage and then to thwart it.

Covert operations: Secret plans and activities carried out by spies and their agencies.

Cyberterrorism: A form of terrorism that seeks to cause disruption by interfering with computer networks.

Democracy: A government elected to rule by the majority of a country's people.

Depleted uranium: One of the hardest known substances, it has most of its radioactivity removed before being used to make bullets.

Dissident: A person who disagrees with an established religious or political system, organization, or belief.

Embargo: A legal prohibition on commerce.

Emigration: To leave one country to move to another country.

Extortion: The act of obtaining money or other property from a person by means of force or intimidation.

Extradite: To surrender an alleged criminal from one state or nation to another having jurisdiction to try the charge.

Federalize/federalization: The process by which National Guard units, under state command in normal circumstances, are called up by the president in times of crisis to serve the federal government of the United States as a whole.

Genocide: The deliberate and systematic destruction of a racial, political, or cultural group.

Guerrilla: A person who engages in irregular warfare, especially as a member of an independent unit carrying out harassment and sabotage.

Hijack: To take unlawful control of a ship, train, aircraft, or other form of transport.

Immigration: The movement of a person or people ("immigrants") into a country; as opposed to emigration, their movement out.

Indict: To charge with a crime by the finding or presentment of a jury (as a grand jury) in due form of law.

Infiltrate: To penetrate an organization, like a terrorist network.

Infrastructure: The crucial networks of a nation, such as transportation and communication, and also including government organizations, factories, and schools.

Insertion: Getting into a place where hostages are being held.

Insurgent: A person who revolts against civil authority or an established government.

Internment: To hold someone, especially an immigrant, while his or her application for residence is being processed.

Logistics: The aspect of military science dealing with the procurement, maintenance, and transportation of military matériel, facilities, and personnel.

Matériel: Equipment, apparatus, and supplies used by an organization or institution.

Militant: Having a combative or aggressive attitude.

Militia: a military force raised from civilians, which supports a regular army in times of war.

Narcoterrorism: Outrages arranged by drug trafficking gangs to destabilize government, thus weakening law enforcement and creating conditions for the conduct of their illegal business.

NATO: North Atlantic Treaty Organization; an organization of North American and European countries formed in 1949 to protect one another against possible Soviet aggression.

Naturalization: The process by which a foreigner is officially "naturalized," or accepted as a U.S. citizen.

Nonstate actor: A terrorist who does not have official government support.

Ordnance: Military supplies, including weapons, ammunition, combat vehicles, and maintenance tools and equipment.

Refugee: A person forced to take refuge in a country not his or her own, displaced by war or political instability at home.

Rogue state: A country, such as Iraq or North Korea, that ignores the conventions and laws set by the international community; rogue states often pose a threat, either through direct military action or by harboring terrorists.

Sortie: One mission or attack by a single plane.

Sting: A plan implemented by undercover police in order to trap criminals.

Surveillance: To closely watch over and monitor situations; the USAF employs many different kinds of surveillance equipment and techniques in its role as an intelligence gatherer.

Truce: A suspension of fighting by agreement of opposing forces.

UN: United Nations; an international organization, of which the United States is a member, that was established in 1945 to promote international peace and security.

Chronology

1607: English colonists settle Jamestown, VA; volunteer militias are founded to defend the community against attacks by Native Americans and, later, the French.

1829: The world's first full-time professional police force, the Metropolitan Police, is set up to enforce law and order in London, England, on the orders of Home Secretary Sir Robert Peel.

1845: The New York Police Department becomes the first modern police force in the United States.

1860s: The first African American officers serve in various police forces.

1910: Alice Stebbins Wells joins the Los Angeles Police Department as the nation's first female police officer.

1919: The Volstead Act imposes prohibition of alcohol, giving extra impetus to the already existing problem of organized crime; in response, police forces are compelled to become more professional, but also more remote from their communities.

1972: The first Neighborhood Watch programs are established on the initiative of the National Sheriffs' Association.

1977: The National Crime Prevention Council (NCPC) is established; it adopts McGruff the Crime Dog as its mascot for a high-profile campaign.

1980s: The work of George L. Kelling popularizes the broken window theory and introduces the idea of zero-tolerance policing.

1985: Teens, Crime, and the Community (TCC) is founded to coordinate crime prevention programs among America's young people.

1994: A new drive seeks to increase police presence at the community level under a major Community Oriented Policing Services (COPS) initiative.

2001: On September 11, terrorists attack the World Trade Center in New York City and the Pentagon in Washington, DC, by crashing aircraft into the buildings.

2002: The NCPC launches a "United for a Stronger America" campaign, aimed at bringing the energies, experience, and organizational skills of crime prevention groups (such as Neighborhood Watch) to help in the war against terrorism at a community level; a "Stop the Hate" campaign is launched to counter rising intolerance in the aftermath of the September 11, 2001, attacks.

2002: The Department of Homeland Security is formed.

2003: First in-car cameras mounted in police and highway patrol vehicles.

2013: National Institute of Justice begins ongoing study of body-worn cameras and law enforcement.

Further Resources

Websites

For the National Crime Prevention Council (NCPC), see: www.ncpc.org

For the Crime Prevention Coalition of America, see: www.crimepreventcoalition.org

For teens, crime, and the community, see: www.nationaltcc.org

For the International Center for the Prevention of Crime, see: www.crime-prevention-intl.org

For the National Neighborhood Watch Association, see www.nnw.org/.

For the National Coalition Against Domestic Violence, see www.ncadv.org/.

Further Reading

Kelling, George L., Catherine M. Coles, and James Q. Wilson. *Fixing Broken Windows: Restoring Order and Reducing Crime in Our Communities.* New York: Free Press, 1998.

Quarantiello, Laura E. *On Guard! How You Can Win the War Against the Bad Guys.* Lake Geneva, WI: Tiare, 1994. This book addresses the problem of crime prevention at household and neighborhood levels.

Sherman, Lawrence W. (ed.). *Evidence-Based Crime Prevention.* New York: Routledge, 2002. This book provides a skeptical overview of current crime prevention policies.

Walker, Samuel. *Sense and Nonsense about Crimes, Drugs, and Communities.* Stamford, CT: Cengage Learning, 2015.

Wilson, James. *Thinking About Crime.* New York: Basic Books, 2013.

Index

About the Author

Michael Kerrigan was born in Liverpool, England, and educated at St. Edward's College, from where he won an Open Scholarship to University College, Oxford. He lived for a time in the United States, spending time first at Princeton, followed by a period working in publishing in New York. Since then he has been a freelance writer and journalist, with commissions across a very wide range of subjects, but with a special interest in social policy and defense issues. Within this field, he has written on every region of the world. His work has been published by leading international educational publishers, including the BBC, Dorling Kindersley, Time-Life, and Reader's Digest Books. His work as a journalist includes regular contributions to the *Times Literary Supplement*, London, as well as a weekly column in the *Scotsman newspaper*, Edinburgh, where he now lives with his wife and their two small children.

About the Consultant

Manny Gomez, an expert on terrorism and security, is President of MG Security Services and a former Principal Relief Supervisor and Special Agent with the FBI. He investigated terrorism and espionage cases as an agent in the National Security Division. He was a certified undercover agent and successfully completed Agent Survival School. Chairman of the Board of the National Law Enforcement Association (NLEA), Manny is also a former Sergeant in the New York Police Department (NYPD) where he supervised patrol and investigative activities of numerous police officers, detectives, and civilian personnel. Mr. Gomez worked as a uniformed and plainclothes officer in combating narcotics trafficking, violent crimes, and quality of life concerns. He has executed over 100 arrests and received Departmental recognition on eight separate occasions. Mr. Gomez has a bachelor's degree and a master's degree and is a graduate of Fordham University School of Law where he was on the dean's list. He is admitted to the New York and New Jersey Bar. He served honorably in the United States Marine Corps infantry.

Picture Credits: 8, Tomas Urbelionis/Shutterstock; 9, White, John H/The U.S. National Archives; 11, pelfophoto/Shutterstock; 12–13, Africa Studio/Shutterstock; 14, Monkey Business Images/Shutterstock; 16–17, Luca De Gregorio/Shutterstock; 19, Maximiliano Ribeiro/Flickr, ChameleonsEye/Shutterstock; 20–21, tommaso79/Shutterstock; 24, Library of Congress; 25, a katz/Shutterstock; 26, Joseph Sohm/Shutterstock; 28, David Burrows/Shutterstock, Kawin Ounprasertsuk/Shutterstock; 29, Chicago Police Department; 31, Kent Sievers/Shutterstock; 32, Gino Santa Maria/Shutterstock; 34, bellena/Shutterstock; 35, a katz/Shutterstock; 36, Library of Congress; 38, Rekindle Photo and Video/Shutterstock; 39, Michael Karlin/Shutterstock; 43, National Crime Prevention Council; 44, Patryk Kosmider/Shutterstock; 46, Laura Bartlett/Shutterstock; 47, Dan Holm/Shutterstock; 48–49, Africa Studio/Shutterstock; 52, Ildar Sagdejev/Wikimedia Commons; 54, Barren-Edmonston Drug Task Force; 56, Jojoo64/Shutterstock; 57, nikamo/Shutterstock; 58–59, Library of Congress; 60, FlyBMW/Shutterstock; 62, KatarzyanBlalasiewicz/iStock; 63, Kekyalyaynen/Shutterstock; 65, Padraic Ryan/Wikimedia Commons; 66, Nyttend/Wikimedia Commons; 67, Adam Jones, Ph.D/Wikimedia Commons; 69, National Crime Prevention Council; 70, Wellmed Charitable Foundation

Cover: kali9/iStock